ULTIMATE
Easy
GUITAR COLLECTION

D1244348

Project Manager: Aaron Stang
Art Layout/Design: Ken Rehm

ARTIST INDEX

CONTENTS

AFTER MIDNIGHT

Words and Music by
J. J. CALE

AQUALUNG

Words and Music by
IAN ANDERSON and JENNIE ANDERSON

Capo at 3rd fret

Moderately slow half-time rock

(Drum fill)

1. 3. Sit - ting on a park bench,
2. 4. Dry - ing in the cold sun,

eye - ing lit - tle girls with bad in - tent.
watch - ing as the fril - ly pant - ies run.

(2nd & 4th times only) Hey, A - qua - lung.

Snot's run - ning down his nose, greas - y fin - gers smear-
Feel - ing like a dead duck, spit - ting out piec - es of his

- ing shab - by clothes. Hey, A - qua - lung.
bro - ken luck. Oh, A - qua - lung.

6

8

bends to pick a dog-end, he goes down to the bog__
go a-way un-eas-y. You poor old sod, you

__ and warms__ his feet.
see it's on - ly me.

1. 2.

E Interlude/Solo:

F Solo: Repeat as needed for solos

G Tempo 1
Verse 5:

Last time

Dee__ dee dee dee,_

ANOTHER BRICK IN THE WALL
(Part 2)

Words and Music by
ROGER WATERS

BAD TO THE BONE

Words and Music by
GEORGE THOROGOOD

1. Now, on the day I was born, the nurs-es all gath-ered 'round,
2. 4. 6. (Inst. solo ad lib....
3. 5. 7. See additional lyrics

and they gazed__ in wide won-der at the joy__ they had found.

The head nurse spoke up; said, "Leave__ this one a-lone."

She could tell__ right a-way I was bad to the bone.

1. 3. 5. 7.

B - b - b - b - b-bad, b - b - b - b - b-bad,

b - b - b - b - b - b - bad,   bad   to the bone.

Verse 3:
I broke a thousand hearts before I met you.
I'll break a thousand more, baby, before I am through.
I wanna be yours, pretty baby, yours and yours alone.
I'm here to tell you, honey, that I'm bad to the bone.
B-b-b-b-b-bad, b-b-b-b-b-bad, b-b-b-b-b-bad,
Bad to the bone.
(To Verse 4/Solo:)

Verse 7:
Now, when I walk the streets, kings and queens step aside.
Every woman I meet, ha ha, they all stay satisfied.
I wanna tell you, pretty baby, what I see I make my own.
And I'm here to tell you, honey, that I'm bad to the bone.
B-b-b-b-b-bad, b-b-b-b-b-bad, b-b-b-b-b-bad,
Bad to the bone.
(To Verse 8/Solo:)

Verse 5:
I make a rich woman beg, and I make a good woman steal.
I make an old woman blush, and I make a young girl squeal.
I wanna be yours, pretty baby, yours and yours alone.
I'm here to tell you, honey, that I'm bad to the bone.
B-b-b-b-b-bad, b-b-b-b-b-bad, b-b-b-b-b-bad,
Bad to the bone.
(To Verse 6/Solo:)

BETH

Words and Music by
PETER CRISS, S. PENRIDGE
and BOB EZRIN

Beth - 2 - 1

BORN TO BE WILD

Words and Music by
MARS BONFIRE

Born to be Wild - 2 - 1

BOTH SIDES NOW

Words and Music by
JONI MITCHELL

Capo at 2nd fret.

Moderately slow

*Original recording in F♯ major.
**Sung octave lower.

Both Sides Now - 2 - 1

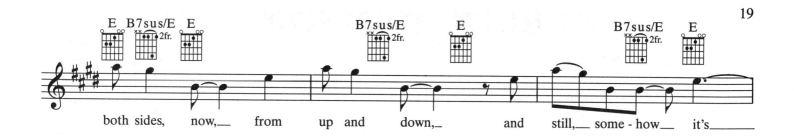

both sides, now,__ from up and down,__ and still,__ some-how__ it's__

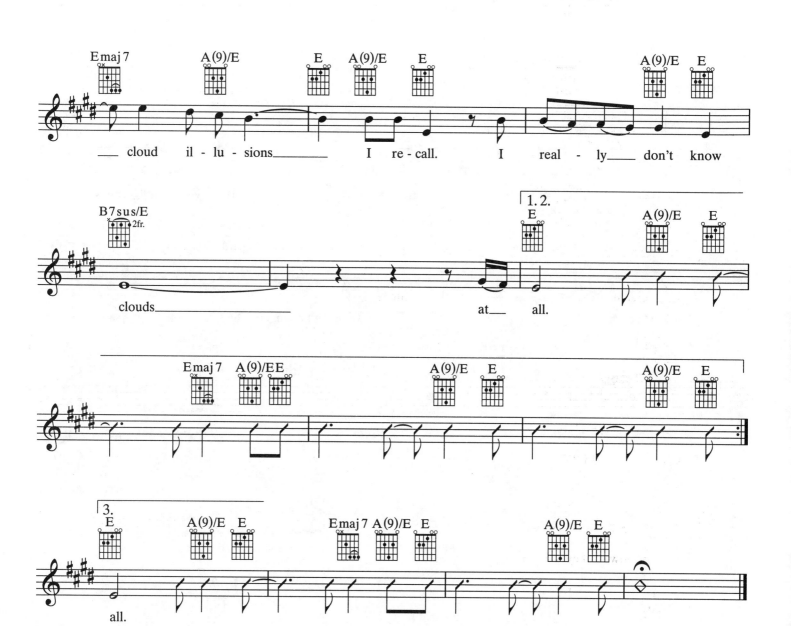

__ cloud il - lu - sions__ I re - call. I real - ly__ don't know

clouds_____ at__ all.

all.

Verse 2:
Moons and Junes and Ferris wheels,
The dizzy dancing way you feel,
As ev'ry fairy tale comes real;
I've looked at love that way.
But now it's just another show;
You leave 'em laughing when you go.
And if you care, don't let them know;
Don't give yourself away.

Chorus 2:
I've looked at love from both sides now,
From give and take, and still somehow
It's love's illusions I recall.
I really don't know love at all.

Verse 3:
Tears and fears and feeling proud,
To say "I love you" right out loud,
Dreams and schemes and circus crowds;
I've looked at life that way.
But now old friends are acting strange;
They shake their heads, they say I've changed.
Well, something's lost but something's gained
In living every day.

Chorus 3:
I've looked at life from both sides now,
From win and lose, and still, somehow
It's life's illusions I recall.
I really don't know life at all.

THE BOYS ARE BACK IN TOWN

Words and Music by
PHIL LYNOTT

*Original recording in A♭ major.

The Boys Are Back in Town - 3 - 1

Verse 2:
You know the chick who used to dance a lot?
Ev'ry night she'd be on the floor shakin' what she got.
Man, when I tell you she was cool, she was red hot.
I mean she was steamin'!
And that time over at Johnny's place,
Well, this chick got up and she slapped Johnny's face.
Man, we just fell about the place.
If that chick don't wanna know, forget her.
(To Chorus:)

Verse 3:
Friday night they'll be dressed to kill
Down at Dino's Bar and Grill.
The drink will flow and blood will spill,
And if the boys wanna fight, you better let 'em.
That jukebox in the corner blastin' out my fav'rite song.
The nights are gettin' warm and it won't be long,
Won't be long till summer comes,
Now that the boys are here again.
(To Chorus:)

CAT'S IN THE CRADLE

Words and Music by
HARRY CHAPIN and SANDY CHAPIN

Cat's in the Cradle - 3 - 1

Cat's in the Cradle - 3 - 2

CALIFORNIA DREAMIN'

By JOHN PHILLIPS and MICHELLE PHILLIPS

* Vocal sung one octave lower.

D.S. % al Coda

Verse 2:
Stopped into a church,
I passed along the way.
Well, I got down in my knees (Got down on my knees.)
And I pretend to pray. (I pretend to pray.)
You know the preacher liked the cold (Preacher liked the cold.)
He knows I'm gonna stay. (Knows I'm gonna stay.)
(To Chorus:)

Verse 3:
All the leaves are brown (All the leaves are brown)
And the sky is gray. (And the sky is gray.)
I've been for a walk (I've been for a walk)
On a winter's day. (On a winter's day.)
If I didn't tell her, (If I didn't tell her,)
I could leave today. (I could leave today.)
(To Chorus:)

CANDLE IN THE WIND

Words and Music by
ELTON JOHN and BERNIE TAUPIN

nev - er know - ing___ who to cling___ to___ when the rain_

___ set in.___ And I would have liked_ to have known_

___ you, but___ I was just___ a kid.___ Your can - dle had burned_ out

long___ be - fore___ your leg - end ev - er did.___

The can - dle had burned_ out long___ be - fore___ your

leg - end ev - er did.___

Verse 2:
Loneliness was tough,
The toughest role you ever played.
Hollywood created a superstar
And pain was the price you paid.
Even when you died,
Oh, the press still hounded you.
All the papers had to say
Was that Marilyn was found nude.
(To Chorus:)

Verse 3:
Goodbye, Norma Jean.
Though I never knew you at all,
You had the grace to hold yourself
While those around you crawled.
Goodbye, Norma Jean,
From the young man in the twenty-second row
Who sees you as something more than sexual,
More than just Marilyn Monroe.
(To Chorus:)

CHANGES

Words and Music by
DAVID BOWIE

ci - nat - ing me.___ Aw, chang - es___ are

tak - ing___ the pace I'm go - ing through. Ch - ch - ch - ch-chang - es,___

I can't trace time._ I said that time may change me,___

but I can't trace time.___

Dm7 Em7 Eb7

Dm7 Dbmaj7 Cmaj7

rit.

Verse 2:
I watch the ripples change their size
But never leave the stream of warm impermanence.
And so the days flow through my eyes,
But still the days seem the same.
And these children that you spit on
As they try to change their worlds
Are immune to your consultations.
They're quite aware what they're going through.
(To Chorus 2:)

Chorus 2:
Ch-ch-ch-ch-changes, (Turn and face the stranger)
Ch-ch-changes.
Don't tell them to grow up and out it.
Ch-ch-ch-ch-changes, (Turn and face the stranger)
Ch-ch-changes.
Where's your shame?
You've left us up to our necks in it.
Time may change me, but I can't trace time.
(To Bridge:)

Chorus 3:
Ch-ch-ch-ch-changes, (Turn and face the stranger)
Ch-ch-changes.
Ooh, look out, you rock and rollers.
Ch-ch-ch-ch-changes, (Turn and face the stranger)
Ch-ch-changes.
Pretty soon now you're gonna get older.
Time may change me, but I can't trace time.

FOR WHAT IT'S WORTH

Words and Music by
STEPHEN STILLS

Verse 2:
There's battle lines being drawn.
Nobody's right if everybody's wrong,
Young people speakin' their minds,
Gettin' so much resistance from behind.
(To Chorus 2:)

Verse 3:
What a field day for the heat,
A thousand people in the street,
Singin' songs and carryin' signs,
Mostly sayin', "Hooray for our side."

Chorus 3:
It's time we stop.
Hey, what's that sound?
Ev'rybody look what's goin' down.

Verse 4:
Paranoia strikes deep,
Into your life it will creep,
It starts when you're always afraid,
Step out of line,
The men come and take you away.

Chorus 4:
We'd better stop.
Hey, what's that sound?
Ev'rybody look what's goin'...

CHINA GROVE

Words and Music by
TOM JOHNSTON

Moderately fast

1.3.

2.4.

1. When the

A Verse:

sun comes up on a sleep-y lit-tle town   down a-round San An - tone

2. See additional lyrics
3. Inst. solo ad lib.

and the folks are ris - in' for an - oth - er day

'round a - bout their homes.   The peo-ple of the town are strange

and they're proud of where they came.

Well, you're
...end solo)

B Chorus:

talk - in' 'bout Chi - na Grove,   whoa,

Verse 2:
Well, the preacher and the teacher, Lord, they're a caution,
They are the talk of the town.
When the gossip gets to flyin' and they ain't lyin'
When the sun goes fallin' down.
They say that the father's insane,
And dear Missus Perkin's a game.
(To Chorus:)

DANNY'S SONG

Words and Music by
KENNY LOGGINS

you bring a tear of joy___ to my eyes,__ and tell me__

ev-'ry - thing___ is gon-na be al - right.__

- thing___ is gon-na be al - right._

Fiddle Solo:

Verse 2:
Seems as though a month ago I was Beta Chi,
Never got high.
Oh, I was a sorry guy.
And now a smile, a face, a girl that shares my name, yeah.
Now I'm through with the game,
This boy will never be the same.
(To Chorus:)

Verse 3:
Pisces, Virgo rising, is a very good sign,
Strong and kind,
And the little boy is mine.
Now I see a family where there once was none.
Now we've just begun,
Yeah, we're going to fly to the sun.
(To Chorus:)

Verse 4:
Love the girl who holds the world in a paper cup.
Drink it up,
Love her and she'll bring you luck.
And if you find she helps your mind, buddy, take her home, yeah.
Don't you live alone,
Try to earn what lovers own.
(To Chorus:)

DO YOU WANT TO KNOW A SECRET?

Words and Music by
JOHN LENNON and PAUL McCARTNEY

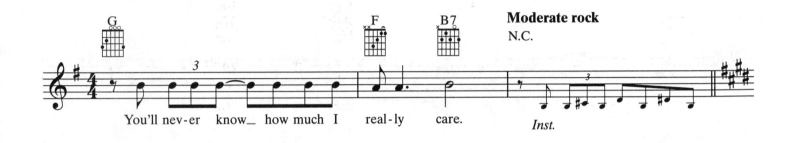

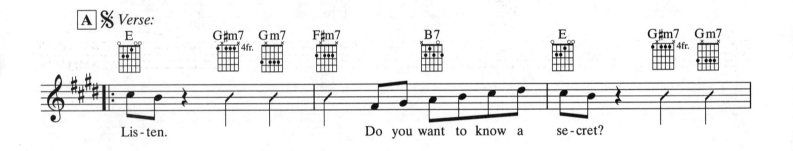

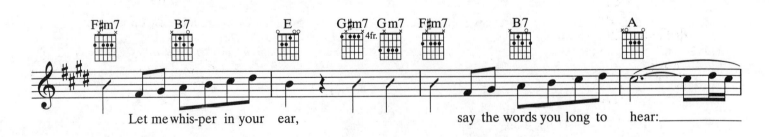

Do You Want to Know a Secret? - 2 - 1

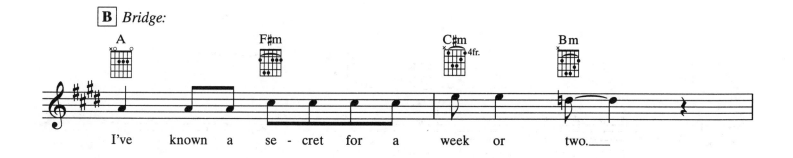

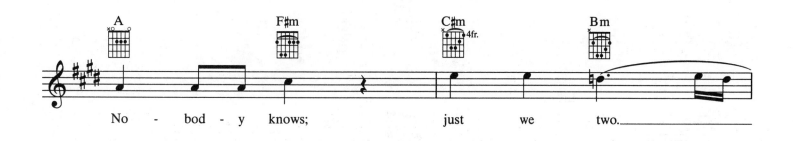

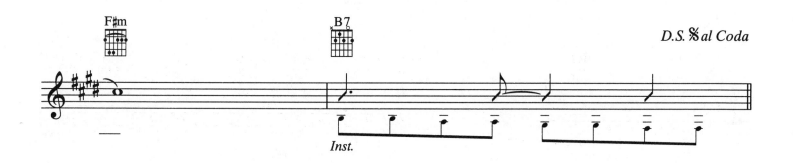

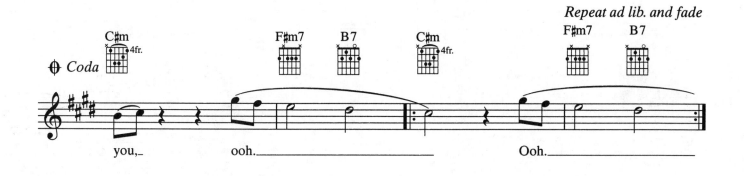

Do You Want to Know a Secret? - 2 - 2

DOWN ON THE CORNER

Words and Music by
JOHN C. FOGERTY

1. Ear - ly in the eve - nin' just___ a-bout sup-per time,___ o - ver by the court - house, they're

2.3. *See additional lyrics*

start-ing to un - wind.___ Four kids on the cor - ner tryin' to bring you up,___

Wil - lie picks___ a tune___ out and he blows it on the harp.

Down on the cor - ner, out here in the street, Wil - lie and the

Verse 2:
Rooster hits the washboard,
People just gotta smile.
Blinky thumps the gut bass
And solos for a while.
Poor-boy twangs the rhythm out,
On his Kalamazoo.
And Willie goes in to a dance
And doubles on kazoo.
(To Chorus:)

Verse 3:
You don't need a penny
Just to hang around,
But if you got a nickle,
Won't you lay your money down.
Over on the corner,
There's a happy noise.
People come from all around
To watch the magic boy.
(To Chorus:)

DRIVE

Capo at 2nd fret.

Words and Music by
RIC OCASEK

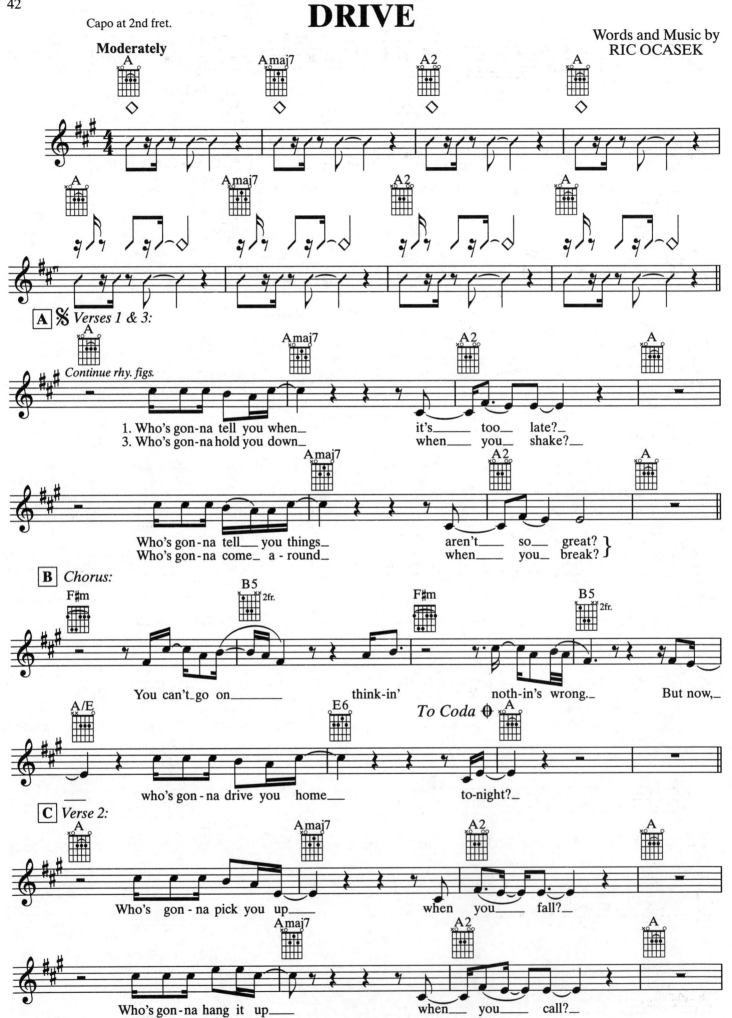

THE FIRST CUT IS THE DEEPEST

Words and Music by
CAT STEVENS

Verse 2:
I still want you by my side,
Just to help me dry the tears that I've cried.
'Cause I'm sure gonna give you a try.
And if you want, I'll try to love again.
Baby, I'll try to love again.
But I know...
(To Chorus:)

FREE BIRD

Words and Music by
ALLEN COLLINS and RONNIE VAN ZANT

1. If I leave here to-mor-row, would you still re-mem-ber me?
2. *See additional lyrics*

Well, I must be trav-el-ing on now,

'cause there's too man-y plac-es I've got to see.

But if I stay here with you, girl, things just could-n't be the same.

'Cause I'm as free as a bird now,

Verse 2:
Bye bye, baby, it's been sweet now,
Though this feeling I can't change.
Please don't take it so badly,
'Cause the Lord knows I'm to blame.
But if I stay here with you, girl, things just couldn't be the same.
'Cause I'm as free as a bird now,
And this bird you cannot change, oh.
And a bird you cannot change,
And this bird you cannot change.
Lord knows, I can't change.
Lord, help me, I can't change.
Lord, I can't change.
Won't you fly, free bird, yeah!

Free Bird - 2 - 2

GO YOUR OWN WAY

Words and Music by
LINDSEY BUCKINGHAM

HOTEL CALIFORNIA

Words and Music by
DON HENLEY, GLENN FREY and DON FELDER

Capo at 7th fret.

Moderate rock

(Play 2nd time only)

A 𝄊 Verse:

1. On a dark des-ert high-way, cool wind in my hair,
2. Her mind is Tif - fan-y twist - ed, she got the Mer - ce - des Benz.
3. *See additional lyrics*

warm_ smell of co-li - tas__ ris - ing up through the air.____
She got a lot of pret-ty, pret-ty boys_ that she calls friends.__

Up a-head in the dis - tance, I saw a shim-mer-ing light.
How they dance in the court - yard, sweet____ sum-mer sweat.

My head grew heav-y and my sight grew dim,_ I had to stop for the night._
Some dance to re - mem - ber, some dance to for - get.__

D.S. 𝄋 al Coda

time_ of year_ (an-y time_ of year_) you can find_it here._   al - i-bis._
nice_ sur-prise,_ (what a nice_ sur-prise_) bring your

Coda

Inst. solo ad lib.

Repeat ad lib. and fade

Verse 3:
Mirrors on the ceiling, the pink champagne on ice.
And she said, "We're all just prisoners here of our own device."
And in the master's chambers, they gathered for the feast.
They stab it with their steely knives, but they just can't kill the beast.
Last thing I remember, I was running for the door.
I had to find the passage back to the place I was before.
"Relax," said the nightman, "We are programmed to receive.
You can check out any time you like, but you can never leave."
(To Coda)

HAVE YOU EVER SEEN THE RAIN?

Written by
J.C. FOGERTY

HEART OF GOLD

Words and Music by
NEIL YOUNG

© 1971, 1972 SILVER FIDDLE MUSIC
Copyrights Renewed
All Rights Reserved

Heart of Gold - 2 - 1

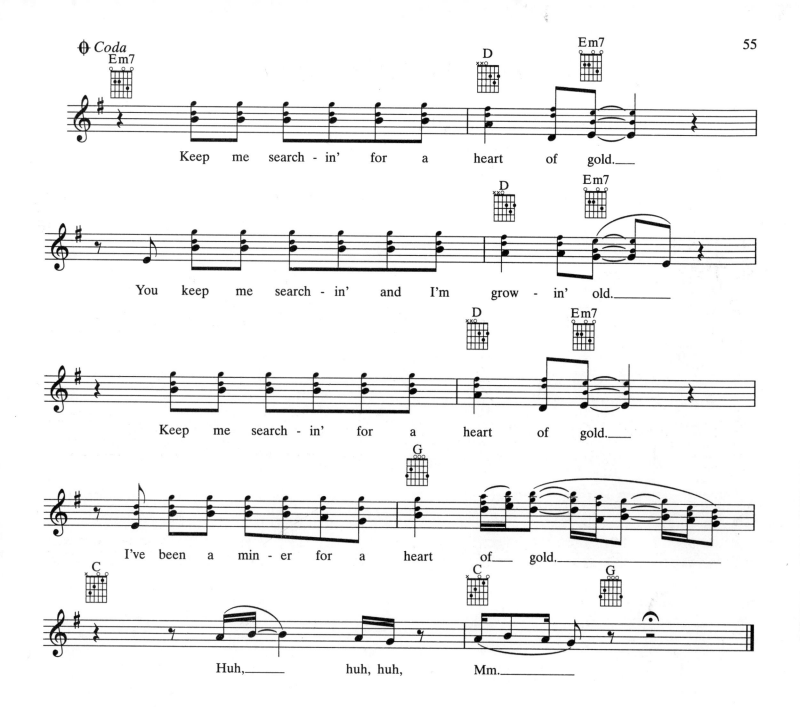

Verse 2:
I've been to Hollywood,
I've been to Redwood.
I'd cross the ocean for a heart of gold.
I've been in my mind, it's such a fine line
That keeps me searchin' for a heart of gold
And I'm gettin' old.
Keep me searchin' for a heart of gold
And I'm gettin' old.
(To Harmonica solo:)

A HORSE WITH NO NAME

Words and Music by
DEWEY BUNNELL

A Horse With No Name - 2 - 1

Verse 2:
After two days in the desert sun,
My skin began to turn red.
After three days in the desert fun,
I was looking at a river bed.
And the story it told of a river that flowed
Made me sad to think it was dead.
(To Chorus:)

Verse 3:
After nine days I let the horse run free
'Cause the desert had turned to sea.
There were plants and birds and rocks and things,
There was sand and hills and rings.
The ocean is a desert with its life underground
And a perfect disguise above.
Under the cities lies a heart made of ground,
But the humans will give no love.
(To Chorus:)

HOUSE AT POOH CORNER

Words and Music by
KENNY LOGGINS

59

House at Pooh Corner - 2 - 2

I KNOW YOU RIDER

TRADITIONAL
Arrangement by GRATEFUL DEAD

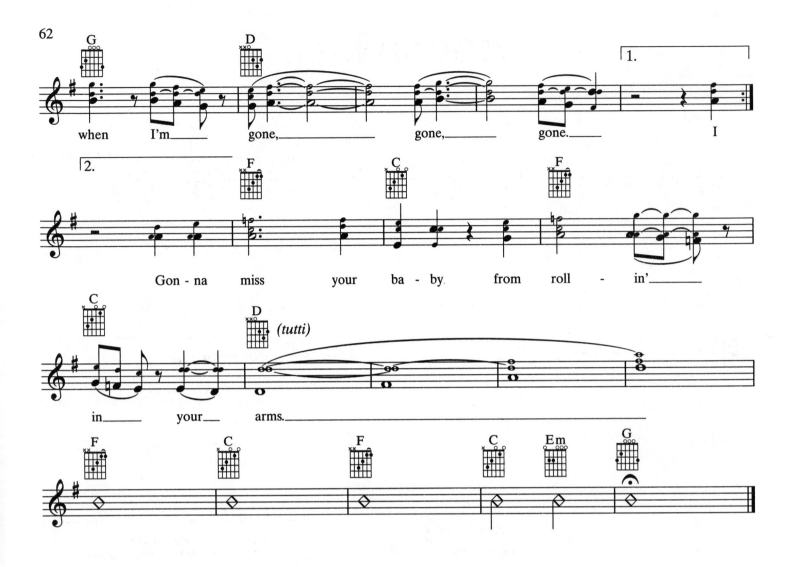

when I'm_____ gone,_____ gone,_____ gone._____ I

Gon - na miss your ba - by. from roll - in'_____

in_____ your_____ arms._____

Verse 4:
I wish I was a headlight on a north-bound train.
I wish I was a headlight on a north-bound train.
I'd shine my light through the cool Colorado rain.
(To Chorus:)

MOONDANCE

Words and Music by
VAN MORRISON

Moondance - 3 - 1

low.
own.
And all the night's_____ mag - ic seems to
And ev - 'ry time I touch___ you, you just

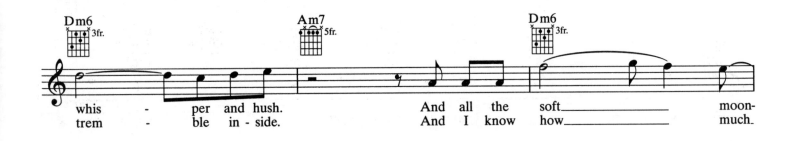

whis - per and hush. And all the soft_____ moon-
trem - ble in - side. And I know how_____ much.

- light seems to shine in your blush. } Can I___
__ you want me that you can't hide. }

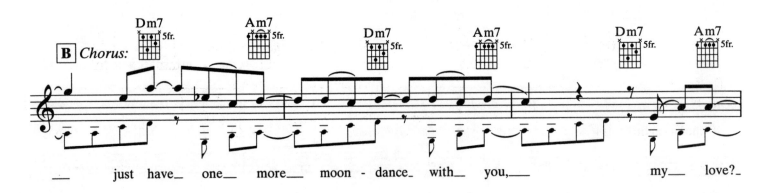

B *Chorus:*

___ just have_ one_ more_ moon - dance_ with_ you,___ my_ love?_

Can I___ just make_ some_ more_ ro - mance_ with_ you,_

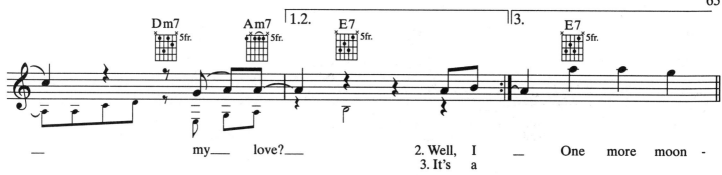

— my love?— 2. Well, I — One more moon -
3. It's a

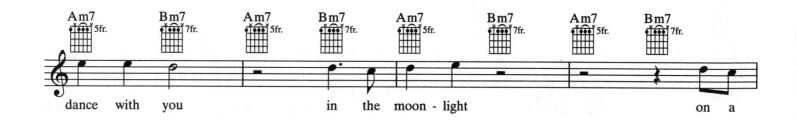

dance with you in the moon - light on a

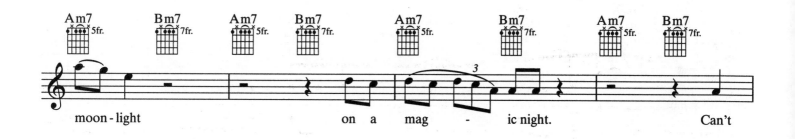

mag - ic night. La la— la— la, in the

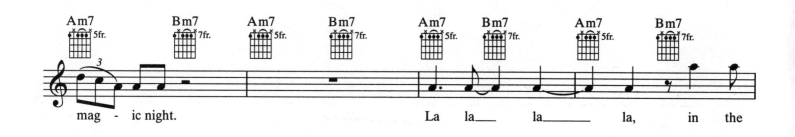

moon - light on a mag - ic night. Can't

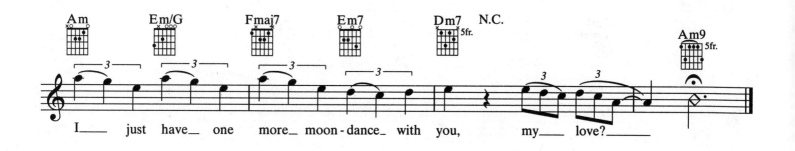

I— just have— one more— moon - dance— with you, my— love?—

Moondance - 3 - 3

I WANT TO HOLD YOUR HAND

Words and Music by
JOHN LENNON and PAUL McCARTNEY

I'D LOVE TO CHANGE THE WORLD

Moderate rock
Intro:

Words and Music by
ALVIN LEE

I'd Love to Change the World - 2 - 1

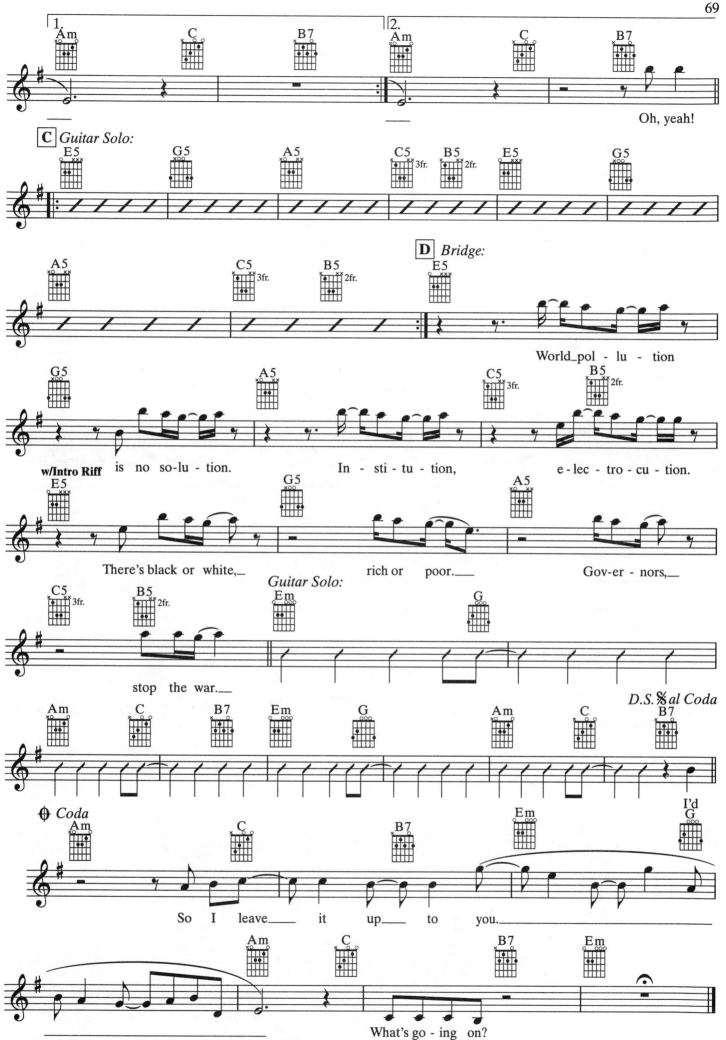

IN-A-GADDA-DA-VIDA

Words and Music by
DOUG INGLE

In - a-gad - da-da-vi - da, hon - ey,   don't you know that I love_____ you?___

In - a-gad - da-da-vi - da, ba - by,   don't you know that I'll al - ways be true?___

Oh, won't you

come with me_____   and a - take my hand._____

Oh, won't_ you come with me_____ and a - walk this

In-A-Gadda-Da-Vida - 2 - 1

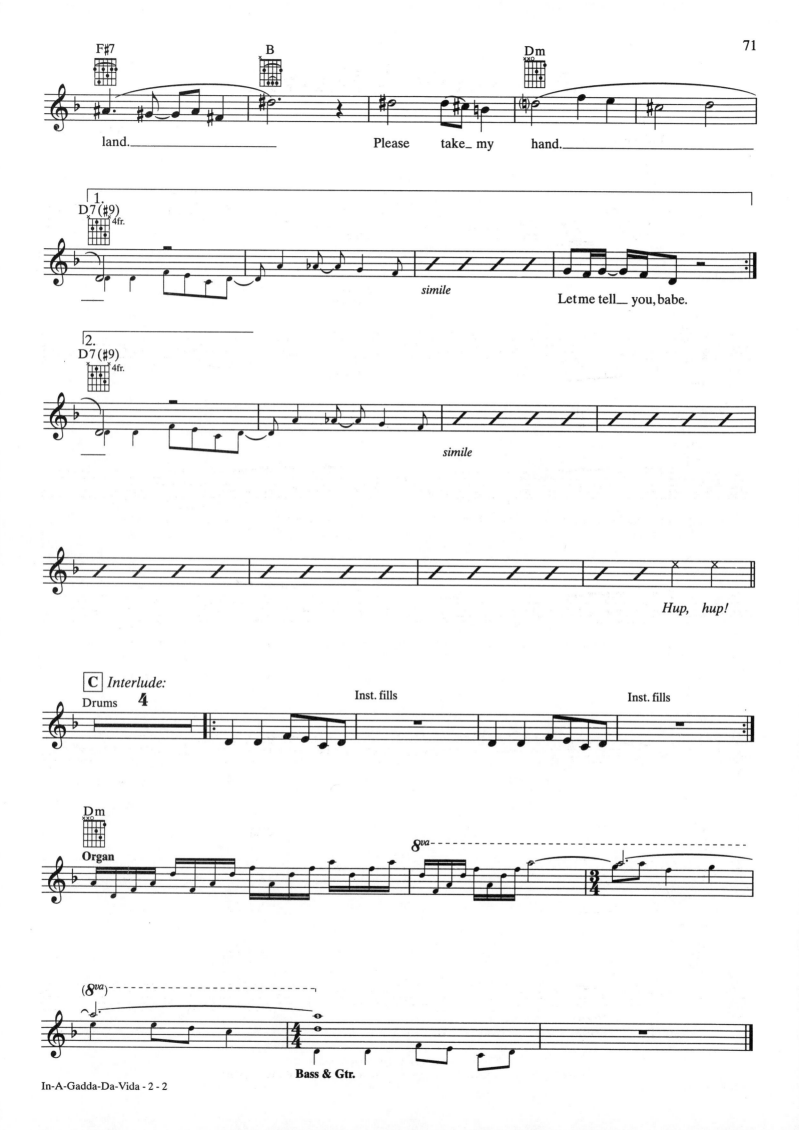

JOSIE

Words and Music by
WALTER BECKER and DONALD FAGEN

LAYLA

Words and Music by
ERIC CLAPTON and JIM GORDON

la,____ dar - lin', won't you ease my wor - ried mind?_____

mind?_____ Lay -

mind?_____

Repeat ad lib. as needed

MARGARITAVILLE

Words and Music by
JIMMY BUFFETT

Verse 2:
Don't know the reason, I stayed here all season
With nothing to show but this brand new tattoo.
But it's a real beauty, a Mexican cutie,
How it got here, I haven't a clue.
(To Chorus:)

Verse 3:
I blew out my flip-flop, stepped on a pop top.
Cut my heel, had to cruise on back home.
But there's booze in the blender, and soon it will render
That frozen concoction that helps me hang on.
(To Chorus:)

MEXICO

Words and Music by
JAMES TAYLOR

Capo at 2nd fret

Moderately

1. Way down here____

A Verse:

____ you need a rea - son to move.__ Feel a fool,_____ run-nin' your state-
2. 3. *See additional lyrics*

- side games.__ Lose your load,__ leave your mind_____ be - hind,__ Ba - by James.

B *Chorus:*

1. Whoa,_____ Mex - i - co,__ it sounds so sim - ple I've just__
2. 3. *See additional lyrics*

____ got to go.__ The sun's so hot, I for-got to go__ home.

Guess I'll have__ to go now._____

Mexico - 2 - 1

Verse 2:
Americano got the sleepy eye,
But his body's still shaking like a live wire.
Sleepy señorita with the eyes on fire.

Chorus 2:
Whoa, Mexico,
You sound so sweet with sun sinking low.
The moon's so bright, like to light up the night.
Make everything all right.

Verse 3:
Baby's hungry and the money's all gone.
The folks back home don't want to talk on the phone.
She gets a long letter, sends back a postcard, times are hard.

Chorus 3:
Whoa, down in Mexico,
I've never really been, so I don't really know.
Whoa, Mexico,
I guess I'll have to go.
(To Coda)

MORE THAN A FEELING

Words and Music by
TOM SCHOLZ

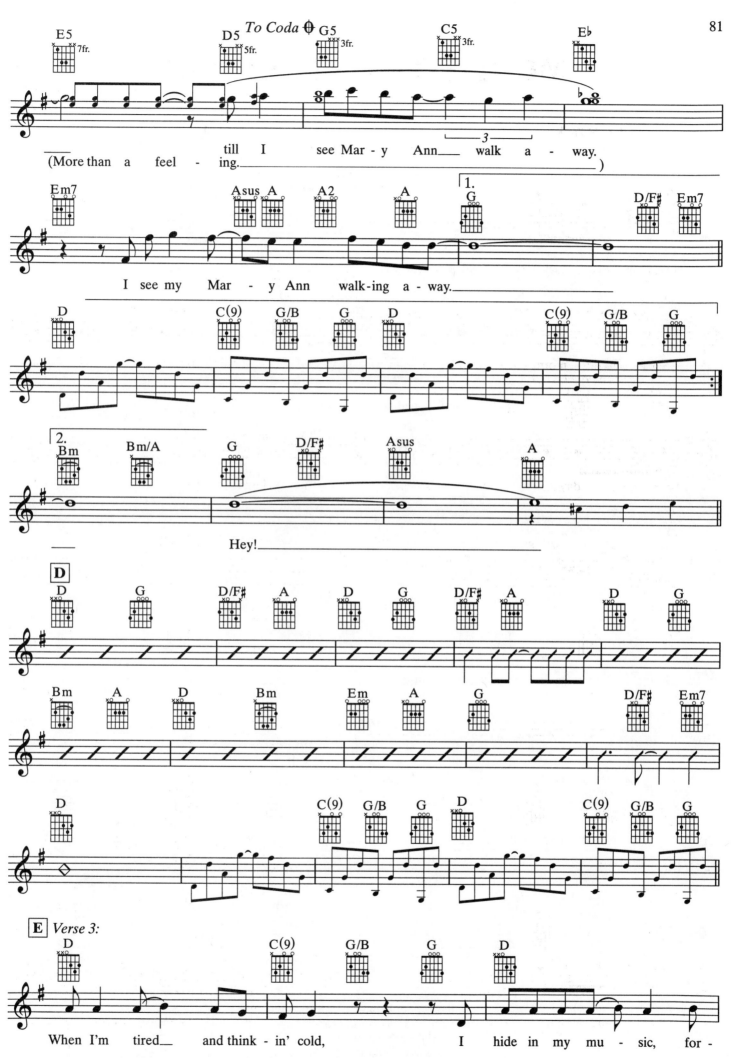

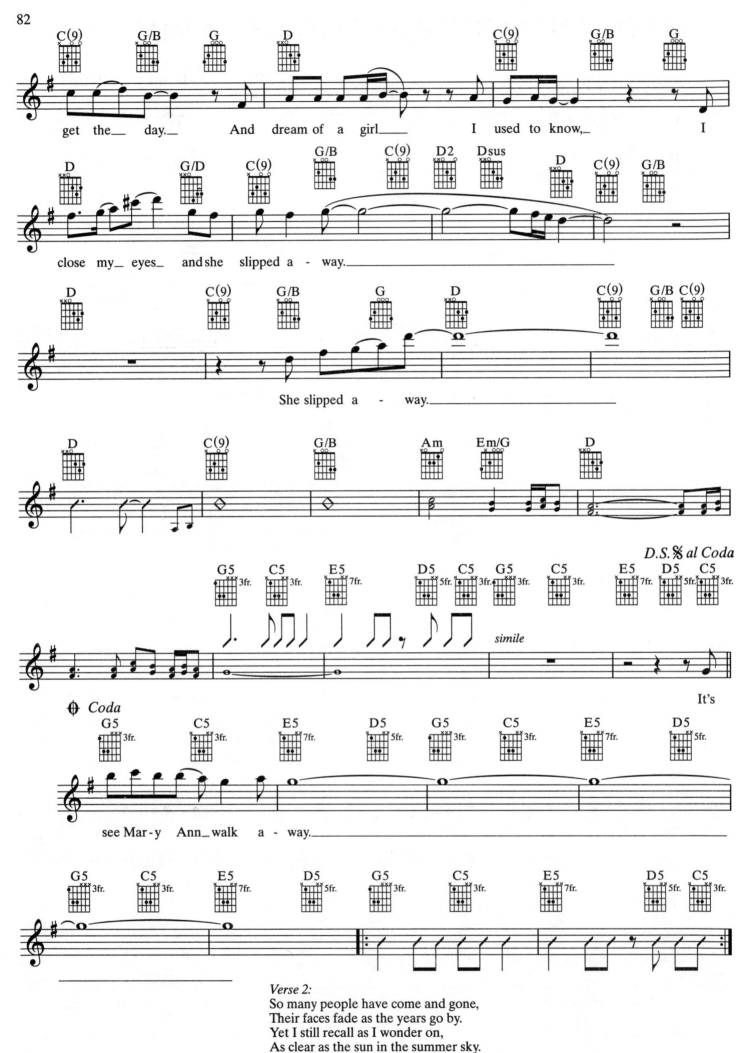

Verse 2:
So many people have come and gone,
Their faces fade as the years go by.
Yet I still recall as I wonder on,
As clear as the sun in the summer sky.
(To Chorus:)

STOP DRAGGIN' MY HEART AROUND

Words and Music by
MICHAEL CAMPBELL and TOM PETTY

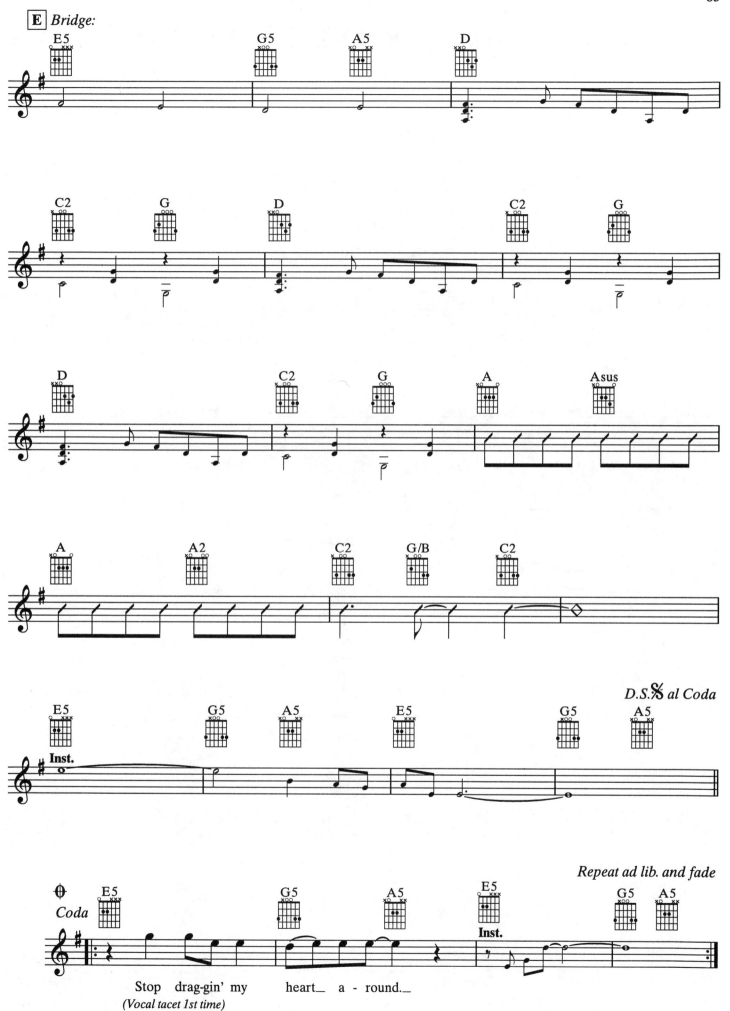

Stop drag-gin' my   heart__ a - round.__
(Vocal tacet 1st time)

NIGHTS IN WHITE SATIN

Words and Music by
JUSTIN HAYWARD

Verse 2:
Gazing at people,
Some hand in hand,
Just what I'm going through
They can't understand.
Some try to tell me
Thoughts they cannot defend.
Just what you want to be
You'll be in the end.
And I love you,
Yes, I love you.
Oh, how I love you.
(To Interlude:)

OLD MAN

Words and Music by
NEIL YOUNG

Verse 2:
Lullabys look in your eyes,
Run around the same old town,
Doesn't mean that much to me
To mean that much to you.
I've been first and last,
Look at how the time goes past,
But I'm all alone at last,
Rollin' home to you.
(To Chorus:)

OLD TIME ROCK & ROLL

Words and Music by
GEORGE JACKSON and THOMAS E. JONES III

Tune down 1/2 step:

⑥ = E♭   ③ = G♭
⑤ = A♭   ② = B♭
④ = D♭   ① = E♭

Moderate rock

N.C.

1. Just take those old rec - ords

A Verse:

G7

off the shelf,___ I'll sit and lis - ten to 'em by my - self.___

2.3.4. See additional lyrics

C7

D7

To - day's mu - sic ain't___ got the same soul,   I like that old   time a -

1.3.

G7

rock and roll.___   2. Don't try to take me to a

2.4.

D7

Still like that old   time a -

B *Chorus:*

G7

rock and roll,___   that kind of mu - sic just soothes the soul.___

C7

D7

I rem - i - nisce a - bout the days of old,___   with that old___ time a -

1.

G7

rock   and   roll.

D7

3. Won't go and hear 'em play a

D.S. 𝄋

Still like that old___ time a - rock and roll,___ that kind of mu - sic just soothes the soul.__ I rem - i - nisce a - bout the days of old,___ with that old_____ time a - rock and roll.___ *Repeat ad lib. and fade* Still like that old___ time a -

Verse 2:
Don't try to take me to a disco.
You'll never even get me out on the floor.
In ten minutes I'll be late for the door.
I like that old time rock and roll.
(To Chorus:)

Verse 3:
Won't go and hear 'em play a tango.
I'd rather hear some blues or funky old soul.
There's only one sure way to get me to go,
Start playing old time rock and roll.

Verse 4:
Call me a relic, call me what you will.
Say I'm old fashioned, say I'm over the hill.
Today's music ain't got the same soul,
I like that old time rock and roll.
(To Chorus:)

PEACEFUL EASY FEELING

Words and Music by
JACK TEMPCHIN

Moderate country rock

A Verse:

1. I like the way your spark - lin' ear - rings lay
2.3. *See additional lyrics*

a - gainst your skin so brown.

And I wan - na sleep with you in the des - ert to - night,

with a bil - lion stars all a - round. 'Cause I got a

B Chorus:

peace - ful eas - y feel - in',

and I know you won't let me down, 'cause I'm

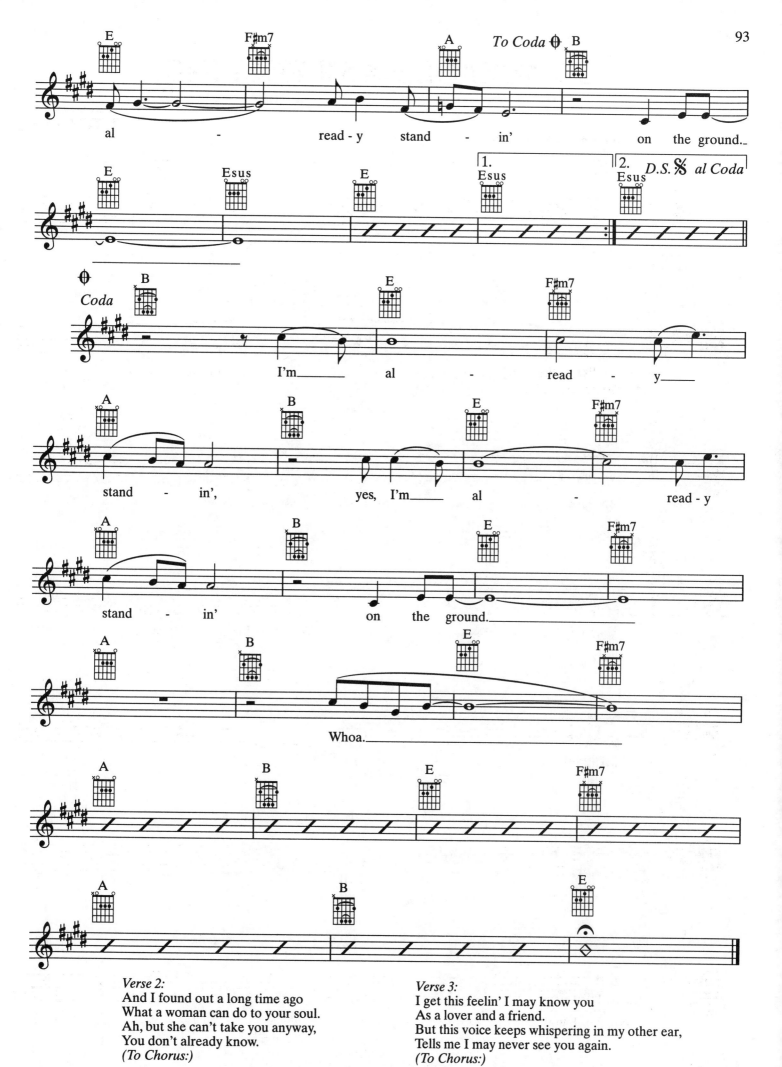

Verse 2:
And I found out a long time ago
What a woman can do to your soul.
Ah, but she can't take you anyway,
You don't already know.
(To Chorus:)

Verse 3:
I get this feelin' I may know you
As a lover and a friend.
But this voice keeps whispering in my other ear,
Tells me I may never see you again.
(To Chorus:)

SAN FRANCISCO
(Be Sure to Wear Some Flowers in Your Hair)

Words and Music by
JOHN PHILLIPS

Verse 2:
For those who come to San Francisco,
Summertime will be a love-in there.
In the streets of San Francisco,
Gentle people with flowers in their hair.
(To Bridge:)

Verse 3:
For those who come to San Francisco,
Be sure to wear some flowers in your hair.
If you come to San Francisco,
Summertime will be a love-in there.
(To Coda)

SUNSHINE OF YOUR LOVE

Words and Music by
JACK BRUCE, PETE BROWN and ERIC CLAPTON

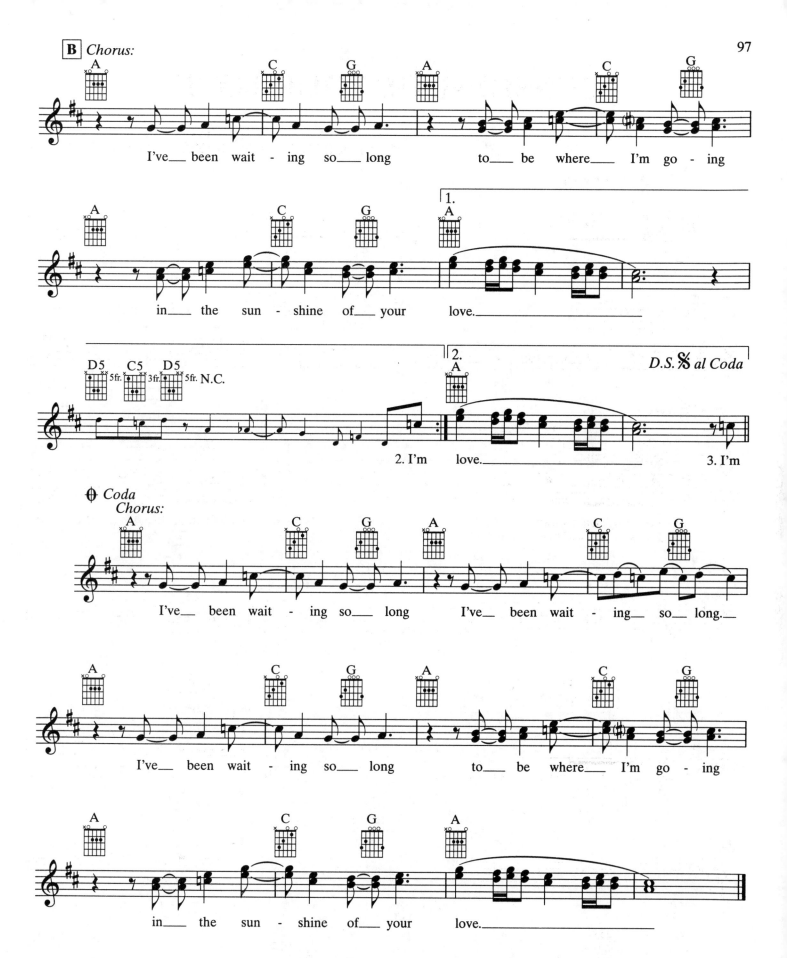

Verses 2 & 3:
I'm with you my love,
The light's shining through on you.
Yes, I'm with you my love,
It's the morning and just we two.
I'll stay with you, darling, now,
I'll stay with you till my seas are dried up.
(To Chorus:)

TEARS IN HEAVEN

Words and Music by
ERIC CLAPTON and WILL JENNINGS

A *Verse:*

1. Would you know my name____ if I saw you in heav - en?
2. 3. *See additional lyrics*

Would it be the same____ if I saw you in heav - en?

I must be strong____ and car - ry on,____ 'cause I know____

To Coda

____ I don't be - long____ here in heav - en.

en.

B *Bridge:*

Time can bring you down,____ time can bend your knees.____

Time can break your heart,__ have you beg - ging please,__ beg-ging please._____

C *Guitar Solo (Verse):*

Be-yond the door__ there's peace I'm sure.__ And I know_

__ there'll be no more__ tears in heav - en.

D.S. 𝄋 *al Coda*

⊕ *Coda*

en. *rit.*

Verse 2:
Would you hold my hand if I saw you in heaven?
Would you help me stand if I saw you in heaven?
I'll find my way, through night and day,
'Cause I know I just can't stay here in heaven.
(To Bridge:)

Verse 3:
Would you know my name if I saw you in heaven?
Would you be the same if I saw you in heaven?
I must be strong and carry on,
'Cause I know I don't belong here in heaven.

Tears in Heaven - 2 - 2

THE NIGHT THEY DROVE OLD DIXIE DOWN

Words and Music by
J. ROBBIE ROBERTSON

The Night The Drove Old Dixie Down - 2 - 1

Verse 2:
Back with my wife in Tennessee,
One day she called to me,
"Virgil, quick come see,
There goes the Robert E. Lee."
Now, I don't mind choppin' wood,
And I don't care if the money's no good.
You take what you need and you leave the rest
But they should never have taken the very best.
(To Chorus:)

Verse 3:
Like my father before me,
I will work the land.
And like my brother above me,
Who took a rebel stand;
He was just eighteen, proud and brave,
But a Yankee laid him in his grave.
I swear by the mud below my feet,
You can't raise a Caine back up when he's in defeat.
(To Chorus:)

TIME OF THE SEASON

Moderately

Words and Music by
ROD ARGENT

© 1967 VERULAM MUSIC CO., LTD. (UK)
Copyright Renewed
All Rights for the U.S.A. and Canada Controlled by MAINSTAY MUSIC, INC.
All Rights Reserved   Used by Permission

Time of the Season - 2 - 1

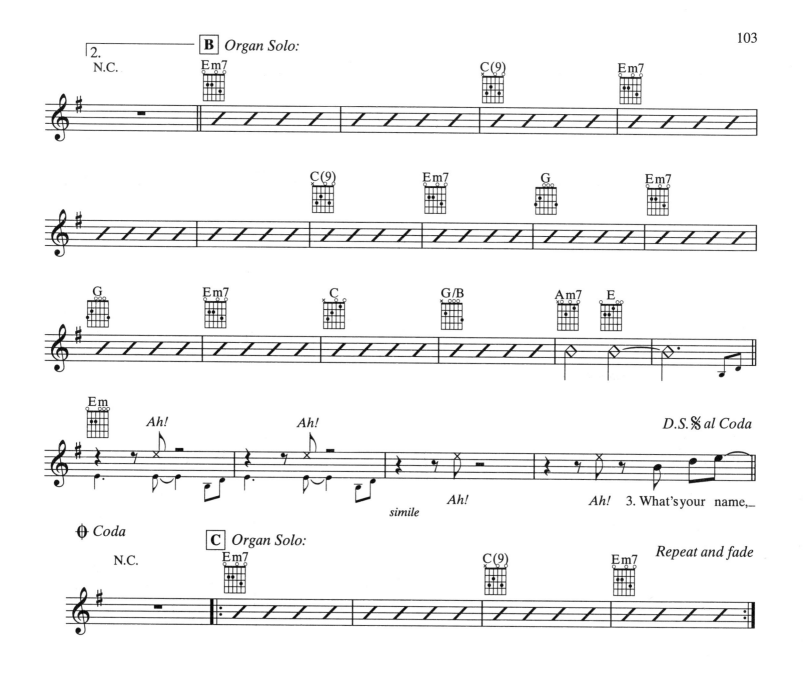

Verses 2 & 3:
What's your name? (What's your name?)
Who's your daddy? (Who's your daddy? He rich?)
Is he rich like me?
Has he taken… (Has he taken…)
Any time (Any time, to show…)
To show you what you need to live?
(Tell it to me slowly.)
Tell you why.
(I really want to know.)
It's the time of the season for loving.
(To Organ Solo:)

WISH YOU WERE HERE

Moderately slow

Words and Music by
ROGER WATERS and DAVID JON GILMOUR

(2nd time add guitar solo)

B *Verse:*

1. So,_____ so you think you can tell_____ heav-en from hell,_

2. *See additional lyrics*

blue skies_ from pain?___ Can you tell a green

field_____ from a cold_ steel rail,_____ a smile_ from a

To Coda

veil? Do you think you can tell?___ Did they get you to trade_

C Bridge:

your he - roes for ghosts,___ hot ash - es for trees,___

hot air___ for a cool___ breeze,___ cold com - fort for change?___

Did you___ ex - change___ a walk-on part__ in the war,__

D.S. % al Coda

for a lead__ role in a cage?___

Coda

Repeat ad lib. and fade

Verse 2:
How I wish, how I wish you were here.
We're just two lost souls swimming in a fish bowl, year after year.
Running over the same old ground, what have we found?
The same old fears, wish you were here.

Wish You Were Here - 2 - 2

YOU REALLY GOT ME

Words and Music by
RAY DAVIES

* Original recording in A♭ major.

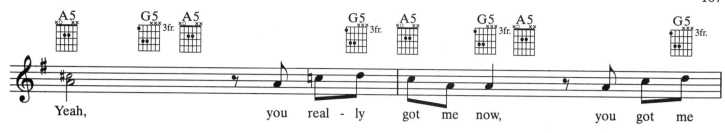

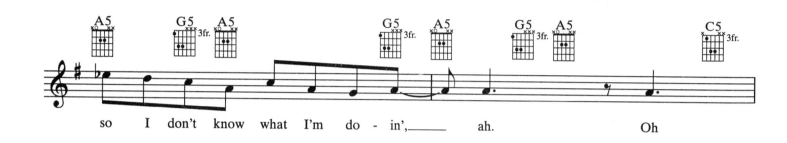

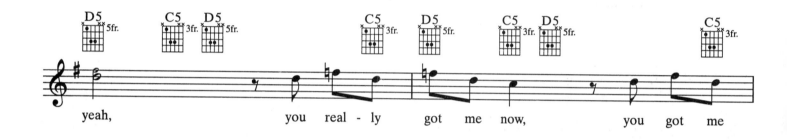

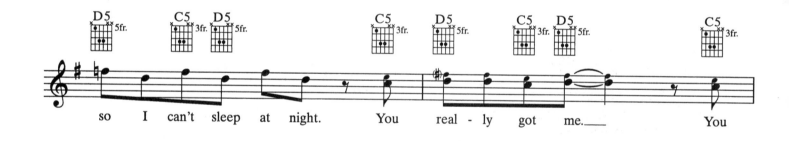

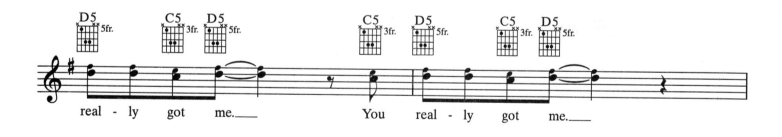

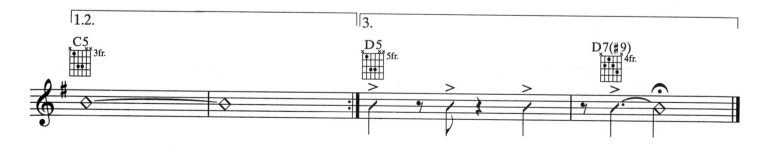

YOUR SONG

Capo at 3rd fret

Words and Music by
ELTON JOHN and BERNIE TAUPIN

Verse 2:
If I was a sculptor, but then again, no,
Or a man who makes potions in a traveling show.
I know it's not much, but it's the best I can do.
My gift is my song and this one's for you.
(To Chorus:)

Verse 3:
I sat on the roof and kicked off the moss,
Well, a few of the verses, well, they've got me quite cross.
But the sun's been quite kind while I wrote this song.
It's for people like you that keep it turned on.

Verse 4:
So excuse me forgetting, but these things I do,
You see, I've forgotten if they're green of they're blue.
Anyway, the thing is, what I really mean,
Yours are the sweetest eyes I've ever seen.
(To Chorus:)

Your Song - 2 - 2

GUITAR TAB GLOSSARY **

TABLATURE EXPLANATION

READING TABLATURE: Tablature illustrates the six strings of the guitar. Notes and chords are indicated by the placement of fret numbers on a given string(s).

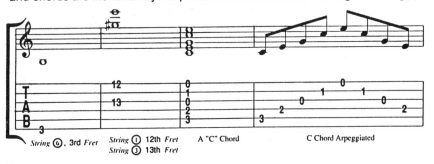

String ⑥, *3rd Fret*   *String* ① *12th Fret*   A "C" Chord   C Chord Arpeggiated
String ③ *13th Fret*

BENDING NOTES

HALF STEP: Play the note and bend string one half step.*

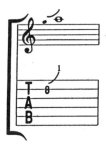

WHOLE STEP: Play the note and bend string one whole step.

WHOLE STEP AND A HALF: Play the note and bend string a whole step and a half.

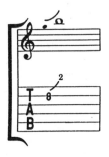

TWO STEPS: Play the note and bend string two whole steps.

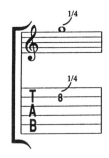

SLIGHT BEND (Microtone): Play the note and bend string slightly to the equivalent of half a fret.

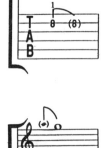

PREBEND (Ghost Bend): Bend to the specified note, before the string is picked.

PREBEND AND RELEASE: Bend the string, play it, then release to the original note.

REVERSE BEND: Play the already-bent string, then immediately drop it down to the fretted note.

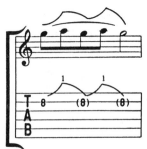

BEND AND RELEASE: Play the note and gradually bend to the next pitch, then release to the original note. Only the first note is attacked.

BENDS INVOLVING MORE THAN ONE STRING: Play the note and bend string while playing an additional note (or notes) on another string(s). Upon release, relieve pressure from additional note(s), causing original note to sound alone.

BENDS INVOLVING STATIONARY NOTES: Play notes and bend lower pitch, then hold until release begins (indicated at the point where line becomes solid).

UNISON BEND: Play both notes and immediately bend the lower note to the same pitch as the higher note.

DOUBLE NOTE BEND: Play both notes and immediately bend both strings simultaneously.

*A half step is the smallest interval in Western music; it is equal to one fret. A whole step equals two frets.

© 1990 Beam Me Up Music
c/o CPP/Belwin, Inc. Miami, Florida 33014
International Copyright Secured   Made in U.S.A.   All Rights Reserved

**By Kenn Chipkin and Aaron Stang

RHYTHM SLASHES

STRUM INDICATIONS: Strum with indicated rhythm. The chord voicings are found on the first page of the transcription underneath the song title.

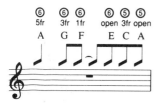

INDICATING SINGLE NOTES USING RHYTHM SLASHES: Very often single notes are incorporated into a rhythm part. The note name is indicated above the rhythm slash with a fret number and a string indication.

ARTICULATIONS

HAMMER ON: Play lower note, then "hammer on" to higher note with another finger. Only the first note is attacked.

LEFT HAND HAMMER: Hammer on the first note played on each string with the left hand.

PULL OFF: Play higher note, then "pull off" to lower note with another finger. Only the first note is attacked.

FRETBOARD TAPPING: "Tap" onto the note indicated by + with a finger of the pick hand, then pull off to the following note held by the fret hand.

TAP SLIDE: Same as fretboard tapping, but the tapped note is slid randomly up the fretboard, then pulled off to the following note.

BEND AND TAP TECHNIQUE: Play note and bend to specified interval. While holding bend, tap onto note indicated.

LEGATO SLIDE: Play note and slide to the following note. (Only first note is attacked).

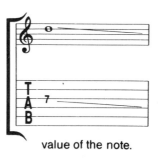

LONG GLISSANDO: Play note and slide in specified direction for the full value of the note.

SHORT GLISSANDO: Play note for its full value and slide in specified direction at the last possible moment.

PICK SLIDE: Slide the edge of the pick in specified direction across the length of the string(s).

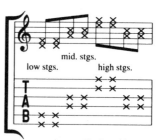

MUTED STRINGS: A percussive sound is made by laying the fret hand across all six strings while pick hand strikes specified area (low, mid, high strings).

PALM MUTE: The note or notes are muted by the palm of the pick hand by lightly touching the string(s) near the bridge.

TREMOLO PICKING: The note or notes are picked as fast as possible.

TRILL: Hammer on and pull off consecutively and as fast as possible between the original note and the grace note.

ACCENT: Notes or chords are to be played with added emphasis.

STACCATO (Detached Notes): Notes or chords are to be played roughly half their actual value and with separation.

DOWN STROKES AND UPSTROKES: Notes or chords are to be played with either a downstroke (⊓) or upstroke (∨) of the pick.

VIBRATO: The pitch of a note is varied by a rapid shaking of the fret hand finger, wrist, and forearm.

HARMONICS

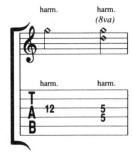

NATURAL HARMONIC: A finger of the fret hand lightly touches the note or notes indicated in the tab and is played by the pick hand.

ARTIFICIAL HARMONIC: The first tab number is fretted, then the pick hand produces the harmonic by using a finger to lightly touch the same string at the second tab number (in parenthesis) and is then picked by another finger.

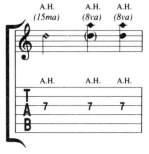

ARTIFICIAL "PINCH" HAR-MONIC: A note is fretted as indicated by the tab, then the pick hand produces the harmonic by squeezing the pick firmly while using the tip of the index finger in the pick attack. If parenthesis are found around the fretted note, it does not sound. No parenthesis means both the fretted note and A.H. are heard simultaneously.

TREMOLO BAR

SPECIFIED INTERVAL: The pitch of a note or chord is lowered to a specified interval and then may or may not return to the original pitch. The activity of the tremolo bar is graphically represented by peaks and valleys.

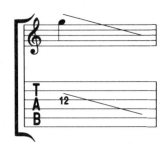

UN-SPECIFIED INTERVAL: The pitch of a note or a chord is lowered to an unspecified interval.